A Corridor of Rain

ANDREA BIANCHI
translated by Silvana Siviero
with a Foreword by Robert Minhinnick

CinnamonPress
INDEPENDENT INNOVATIVE INTERNATIONAL

Published by Cinnamon Press
Meirion House
Glan yr afon
Tanygrisiau
Blaenau Ffestiniog
Gwynedd
LL41 3SU
www.cinnamonpress.com

The right of Andrea Bianchi to be identified as author of this work has been asserted by him in accordance with the Copyright, Designs and Patent Act, 1988. Copyright © 2011 Andrea Bianchi
ISBN: 978-1-907090-28-8
British Library Cataloguing in Publication Data. A CIP record for this book can be obtained from the British Library.

All rights reserved. No part of this publication may be reproduced, stored in a retrieval system, or transmitted in any form or by any means, electronic, mechanical, photocopying, recording or otherwise without either the prior written permission of the publishers. This book may not be lent, hired out, resold or otherwise disposed of by way of trade in any form of binding or cover other than that in which it is published, without the prior consent of the publishers.

Designed and typeset in Palatino by Cinnamon Press. Cover design by Cottia Fortune-Wood from original artwork ', agency © Dreamstime.com
Printed in Poland
Cinnamon Press is represented in the UK by Inpress Ltd www.inpressbooks.co.uk and in Wales by the Welsh Books Council www.cllc.org.uk.
The publisher acknowledges the financial assistance of the Welsh Books Council.

Acknowledgments

Andrea Bianchi and Silvana Siviero are particularly grateful to Robert Minhinnick for his advice and support. Some of these poems appeared in the Spring issue 2008 of *Poetry Wales*.

Contents

Foreword by Robert Minhinnick	5
Truer than the Door Itself	13

Rooms, Meadows & Missed Appointments

On The Ottoman	17
The Chandelier	18
Bow Stretched Precariously	19
The Painting	20
Twilight	21
In The Window	22
Red Brown Green Overflowing	23
Out of the Morning	24
The Room Continues	25
From The Train	26
Wide Open and Blue	27
Between Icy Uphill Roads	28
Backlighting	29
Prickly Grey All	30
The Meadow over the Roofs	31
August	32
Like Corks Floating Downstream	33
Grey Silence	34
Pale Crescent-shaped Moons	35
Intimate Companionship	36
The Bench	37
Sound Leaves Silence	38
The Usual Light	39
Eight Lamp Posts	40
I Am a Corridor of Rain	41
Going Downhill	42
I Give a Glance	43

Movement & Moments, Charcoal & Colour
   Barbed Wire   47
   Skittles   48
   Seagulls like Pieces of Burnt Paper   49
   The Rat and the Nightingale   50
   Movement   51
   The Thick Black Water   52
   Stones like Stars   53
   Umbrella - Clouds over Lofty Heads   54
   Slow and Slower   55
   Running   56
   The Fireplace   57
   Cobbled Road   58
   Cold over the Digging Site   59
   Plucked By the Wind   60
   A Little More Than Mist   61
   The Lovers   62
   The Square   63
   Rust Iron Freshness   64
   Dotted With Pebbles   65
   Pale Eyes   66
   Crows Black Edges   67
   Heavy Cart   68
   It Draws Strength From   69
   In The Old Yellow Paint   70
   Enamel in Motion   71
   Story of One   72
   Vertigo on the Ground   75

Notes   80
Biographical Note   80

Foreword

Exact contemporaries, Andrea Bianchi and Silvana Siviero were born within five days of one another in 1960, in Torino and south Wales respectively.

They first met in school in 1973 after Silvana returned to Italy, and since 1997 have created an extraordinarily creative and ambitious literary partnership.

Andrea Bianchi is a poet in Italian, who has published four volumes of his own writing. 'A Corridor of Rain' is his first collection in English, translated by Silvana and himself.

Bianchi tells me he has never studied George Oppen, but reading these translations I am reminded of the essay, 'The Mind's Own Place', especially when Oppen writes: *Modern American poetry begins with the determination to find the image, the thing encountered, the thing seen each day, whose meaning has become the meaning and the colour of our lives. Verse, which had become a rhetoric of exaggeration, of inflation, was to the modernists, a skill of accuracy, of precision, a test of truth.*

Yes, accuracy and precision are what we find in this book, close observations of the physical world and how it uplifts or tortures the spirit. It is as if Bianchi's poems are telling us 'here is something I have looked at or thought of a thousand times. But at last I have truly *seen* or *understood* it. At last.'

Thus this collection might be viewed as a series of epiphanies, or at least moments of illumination and comprehension (Oppen's *meaning?*) in the most ordinary of circumstances or environments. At last the meaning intrudes. It insists. It will not be unmeant. And this meaning cannot be lost in the modern world's atrocity of noise and dependence on unmeaning.

Andrea Bianchi is revealed in these short, sometimes cryptic lyrics as very much his own man. Yet, when I read

'A Corridor of Rain' I recall the Breton poet, Guillevic, who composed in French. Guillevic's 'The Flame' (a poem unknown to Bianchi) is a testament of what its writer believes. That 'flame' is also 'meaning'. It 'lives and moves'

> *In the piece of zinc, the cupboard door,*
> *the pencil, the clock, and the wine in the glass,*
> *in the tobacco jar, the stove's enamel,*
> *the paper on the table and the clean clothes,*
> *in the iron of the hammer, in the copper piping,*
> *in your crossed knees, your most hidden places.*

Guillevic discovers sensibility or 'meaning' in 'things' such as a 'wardrobe', 'a nail', 'a bowl', or in geometric figures (a 'trapezoid', a 'right angle') where surely there can be none. The sensibility Guillevic is describing is of course his own as he meditates on his subjects. Guillevic is looking into his own mind, as Bianchi does in poems such as 'I am a Corridor of Rain' when he gazes hard at seemingly mundane objects and discovers wonder. Or, at the very least, makes his reader wonder.

> *I am a corridor of rain*
> *made of houses,*
> *I paint the dark streets*
> *with bands of light.*
> *The pale grey morning*
> *rolled up in my cloudy depths*
> *not over the sea.*
> *Fishermen unload silvery blades,*
> *or so it seems.*

Bianchi has found the courage to mythologise his own experience. Thus he trusts his perceptions, fleeting or hard-won, and understands the inestimable value of their importance. He abjures 'exaggeration' and 'inflation' and frequently challenges us with a stark presentation of 'facts'. At other times he shows little inclination to construct a central image, and instead contents himself with musings peripheral or 'tangential'. *'Story of One'* and *'Vertigo on the Ground'* give evidence to this. Indeed, throughout this book, more is hinted at than revealed. Significantly, the predominant colours are 'grey' or 'palegrey'.

Yet, as Maurizio Pallante writes in the Introduction to *La stanza prosegue (The Room Continues),* Andrea Bianchi 'manages to grasp unusual and mysterious links beyond the apparent appearance of things.' Certainly he reveals to us what we might never have guessed. And it is this characteristic that dominates *A Corridor of Rain* via cleverly abbreviated descriptions, and sudden impressions which 'explain' even as they challenge. Indeed it is from Bianchi's descriptions of silence that we learn about his world of sound, from his depictions of absence that we glimpse the presence of his people.

Guillevic addresses a cherry-tree thus: *Here you are in reality / as you were dreamed,* while Bianchi writes

> *Holding the pen under my nose*
> *I saw lights,*
> *lights in the steel,*
> *quick white intense in the pen.*
> *Wine in my stomach,*
> *the world light,*
> *stones in the streets,*
> *stones like stars.*
>   *'Stones like Stars'*

and:

And it is the light over the stairs,
the usual light
before night falls on the courtyard
mingling trees and cars.
And it is the light over the stairs,
the usual light of old memories,
of deep thoughts,
illuminating
without colouring.
    'The Usual Light'

Andrea Bianchi has said that 'I dedicated twelve years to translating poets and prose writers and I learned to love their poems and short stories and novels. But poetry, for me, is always that powerful and mysterious voice of my childhood.'

This is a poetry that is clearly indebted to other art forms—painting and music especially. Bianchi has written, 'my beginning was without books, but full of sound.' Certainly in this book we discover both childish astonishment and the pangs of a more general alienation from an inexplicable urban world.

Robert Minhinnick

In memory of Aunt Elena

This silence
this side of the window
reminds me of Aunt Elena's

the dark afternoons
the fresh corners
the brief sound of
    the coffee-spoon on
        the small cup
and
the rain outside
in the concrete courtyard.

A Corridor of Rain

Truer than the Door Itself

When your eyes do not see what they should see but something else, when they search and, thanks to a series of details they normally neglect, come to catch just that thing they had never seen (now revealing itself different, dumb or differently eloquent similar to a closed treasure casket), then we have had a vision that does not go as far as being a revelation: only the mystery of the world is asserted, as nothing can be revealed. I have these 'useless' visions that nurture me as a poet, that make me a poet; and when my eyes look without seeing but only spotting some insubstantial something, that something will immediately guide me, my senses, in view of Poetry, never in view of the Truth.

What has just been said is a preliminary statement to a refusal: I will never tell the story of a man but for the colour of his new shoes; I will never tell a lie but for the strange sound the words have in composing it; I will never know it is Sunday tomorrow but for that fine air on certain Saturday evenings, or that I've finally returned home but for that particular scratch in that particular point on the door, truer than the door itself, truer than the name I am now signing with:

Andrea Bianchi

Rooms, Meadows &
Missed Appointments

On the Ottoman

Against the dark red of the velvet
the black shape of the nose,
the hand folded as a shell,
the apricot creases of the sweater
with its threadbare cloth
and the train of buttons
feet at the bottom, big.
In the slightest glimmer
dusk dilates the pupils,
all colours fade.

The Chandelier

Sliding across ceiling and walls
in the form of seedpods and spear points,
narrowing widening softening pale grey,
spreading crisscrossing covering with a grid
the nude bathers of Renoir.
Like goblets and terraces
opening as wide as flowers.
They limit the yellow.
And widening sliding they repeat
the shadows of its thin arms.

Bow Stretched Precariously

It does not follow the pattern on the dresser
the wooden board
of a strange nature.
It encloses human forms
and tells a story.
The black crystal set cuts itself out
bombé-like;
ancient photos are like windows
without shutters;
instruments on the top:
mandolin mandola violin,
bow stretched precariously
on the embroidered leaves of the curtain:
curling falling turning
embroidering the scanty light.

The Painting

Up to the sky and higher than the hills
the gentian hangs onto the sofa.
The big green marble-like leaves
crossed by swollen veins
making clear-cut shadows.
Yellow flowers on faraway pines
creating a dwarf's face
in the top corner.
The biggest leaf is cut
right out of the white edge,
close to me
as if I were on the ground,
as if it were touching my face.

Twilight

Thread of gold around the oval of the shiny
table top furrowed by shadows,
by lights.
Finishing sharply it cuts soft folds
the same as heavy antique colours,
pale, far ones,
small, unobtrusive ones,
opening smooth sharp
round spaces
tinged with golden threads
where the white lights up the hill.

In the Window

Tangle of iron,
of rust plastic dust,
corners cut by thin shadows
by stretched lines
on empty balconies.
Opposite a house three narrow windows
with half shutters
sharply stretching the shadows.
In the early morning of dark movements,
dull colours on red roofs
where aerial arms
do not glow.

Red Brown Green Overflowing

Red buildings on the compact surface,
streets sloping down like sparks
from the avenue,
from the middle of the building,
strange and twisted they swarm
where the flowing of the lights
is at its thickest among bare branches.
Bent plants gathered in a corner:
red brown green overflowing
from the white fence
at the margin of the movement.

Out of the Morning

The light traces new courses.
Where the window gives onto the stairs
quiet greys of rain
cross the concrete courtyard.
Spaces fade away
among crystal pinnacles
in the white glare:
the frame shines for a moment
and the rough transparent glass slides
suddenly locking me
out of the morning.

The Room Continues

The room continues
in the red enamel of the vase,
through the depth of the drawing,
in shadows, in lights, in sounds,
through and beyond
a bright line moving in the night,
painted on the ceiling,
filtered through the shutter
capturing its essence.
Down from the cat's dreams,
fall streetlights and rain,
if it rains.
The mute sun
giving its light,
taking shadows from the cat.

From the Train

I see taut wires tracing
clear parallels:
now tightening crossing
now widening reducing
in the fog.
Down below rigid
runs the railway.
Dark masses slipping past.
Here and there lights sparkling
breaking
far away.
And the noise rocking me
from grey to grey
a drum beat leading
to the coming morning.

Wide Open and Blue

     Wide open and blue
     the house peels
     its walls
     off the pale swollen
     green
stretching out onto the pebbles
     onto the dirty gleaming tracks
of the ballast.

Between Icy Uphill Roads

On the sloping meadow
like on a white board
a stack of wood
and four houses,
frost on the contours,
now more rigid,
between icy uphill roads
and downhill roads,
the slanting
red fronted houses
overlooking the railway.

Backlighting

The flat stream a small rectangle
made of stones,
speckled with white,
compressed in the concrete.
Black leaves
against hazes of light.
The trunk standing out.
The man climbing onto the bridge,
hay on his shoulders:
his foot lifted
compressed in the glare.

Prickly Grey All

Lying in the meadow,
made blacker by the cold,
taut broken by the silver downpour,
thin little trees
climb up through heavy rain.
Tangle of bare branches
and fence planks,
prickly grey all
the meadow sloping leaning
against the walnut tree trunk,
against the white wall.

The Meadow over the Roofs

Black in the centre,
two balconies underneath.
Irregular strings of light
emphasize edges,
mountain house corners,
difficult patterns.
The meadow over the roofs,
a tight rough sky,
distinct like the light
in the irregular shade.

August

I am tired,
the day is tired
and the light.
Thicker the colours
and more solid,
with few shades.
Monotonous the day
inviting you to sleep,
a sweet sleep.
You long to sleep
for a long time,
hoping for rain,
for the wind to break the heat.

Like Corks Floating Downstream

On the rain and asphalt
of the provincial road,
thinking of Baudelaire's poems,
I saw the old yellow-beard Balbal
magically appearing out of thin air.
On the margin of the time
I spent at the church
waiting was like mornings,
opening slowly,
curtains never clear never calm,
like corks floating downstream.

Grey Silence

Bending down in a corner
I spy on the low morning
that holds the rain
like an unexpressed feeling;
I spy on the grey silence
that longs for the damp brown,
and for my blood;
I spy on the silent spot
in the leaden morning.

Pale Crescent-shaped Moons

Little crescent-shaped wall:
on it a striped cat
riffled by the wind mingling
with the sliding light
of an approaching storm.
Architectural motifs engraving the air,
streetlights standing out like tinplated hats;
treetops bending
tearing the tender leaves:
they are not experiments,
pale crescent-shaped moons mean little,
nothing I do not already know.
Feeling satisfied between chimney pots and sloping roofs,
I feign smiles at the outburst of the swallows.

Intimate Companionship

Intimate companionship is a maze of roads,
strange if the light is deceptive,
softened with the passing of time,
engraved with signs when dawn
betrays itself in sleep.
From above every edge sounding like a song,
deeper and more welcoming
than the rashest smile,
every line every game
is repeated forever.
Then boredom creeps up on you:
a cobweb of shadows.

The Bench

Curved metal legs
sinking in gravel,
bolts joining the green axle
to rusty metal,
equally fixed its back,
other solitudes scratched on it:
the bench.

Sound Leaves Silence

Can two or four wings
encircled by colours
sink into the air with the lights?
and the first raindrops?
and the evening reflections?
Sound leaves silence
when it moves away,
a black void
and fear…

The Usual Light

And it is the light over the stairs,
the usual light
before night falls on the courtyard
mingling trees and cars.
And it is the light over the stairs,
the usual light of old memories,
of deep thoughts,
illuminating
without colouring.

Eight Lamp Posts

There are eight lamp posts,
grey like words
full of light,
there are eight
on the sea,
eight drops of mercury
on the concrete pier.
Air over the sea
and the dog splashing
and the girl's thin chest.
Eight crystal spheres I see
in the sun:
between people walking
I count the lamp posts.

I Am a Corridor of Rain

I am a corridor of rain
made of houses,
I paint the dark streets
with bands of light.
The pale grey morning
rolled up in my cloudy depths
not over the sea.
Fishermen unload silvery blades,
or so it seems.

Going Downhill

Nightlights
inside my weariness,
downhill to the river,
to the church,
to the ink-water,
to my longing to sail
the drama of dreams.

I Give a Glance

I give a glance
at the sea
at the side of the dressing-table
between the silver mirror
and the duvet bed muzzle

curtains with black eyes
    bronze tails
swords in the back
    in the bronze.

Movement & Moments,
Charcoal & Colour

Barbed Wire

Sparrows trace arabesques in the air
between rusty barbed wires,
thick with iron thorns:
on the wall
at noon
a breath of wind
raises the dust on the land.

Skittles

By the movement of wings
a passage opens
in the thick afternoon
of hazel-brown brushstrokes,
of shredded clouds:
skittles falling
always
in silence.

Seagulls like Pieces of Burnt Paper

Not silver splinters
but birds,
seagulls like pieces of burnt paper,
flying in the fire making a rhythm
making a sound:
explosions of tongues of fire,
of orange, of yellow.
A ship is leaving the port
and people wave:
fishing boats will go out tonight.

The Rat and the Nightingale

A squeak:
a metallic voice
breaking like a sharp angle,
interrupting the dull sounds
of the common language,
constant over the surface of the water,
over the delicate bodies lying in the sun.
The quiet scratching of a frightened rat
gnawing through the silences
between the nightingale's songs.

Movement

Limbs and words mingling
in sandy games,
small shadows of sand dunes,
long shadows of beach umbrellas,
intersecting
with bright striped sails
with wind scent
from remote seas,
with people's continuous milling
with different voices ringing,
watching a small animal
covering itself with sand
in a shell of sun.

The Thick Black Water

The thick black water
turning like small walls
around dark posts of rotten wood
covers neither the legs of the Japanese,
nor the orange peel.
The thick black sand
covers neither the white
ship out there
on the horizon,
nor the worn-out shoe,
nor the broken heel
of the stiletto.

Stones like Stars

Holding the pen under my nose
I saw lights,
lights in the steel,
quick white intense in the pen.
Wine in my stomach,
the world light,
stones in the streets,
stones like stars.

Umbrella-clouds over Lofty Heads

after Georges Seurat's 'Sunday Afternoon on the Island of Grand Jatte'

Umbrella-clouds over lofty
heads
haphazardly set to soar.

>Featureless faces
>warm between the top hats
>and the plumed hats.

Small figures
appearing out of the thicket
with small umbrellas.

>The merging of
>dark dresses
>gestures
>water blue.

Slow and Slower

Slow and slower
like a greyer colour
the afternoon dies away.
Children playing and hiding
in rusty lanes and mountain homes.
Stones in the wall grey,
heavy, dry, uneven,
jutting out like steps.
Men crossing the bridge
looking at the white water on the stones.
No leaf without a still
drop holding the light.
Rain gathering
in the stone shadow.

Running

Running red

> tin edges
> chirping yellow
> eyeless houses

running green

> crushed thicket
> confused depth
> grey throbbing
> of tight jackets.

The Fireplace

...on which an oil
lamp found in a ditch
is hanging...from which
    the rough wood of a
    beam driven in the stormy
    wall is widening...for which
        the fireplace is
        deep
        with its brass dragon
        perching...

Cobbled Road

The road suddenly changes:
cobbles running tangential to the bend
the pavement traces,
ending at the indefinite, white
edge.
Our legs bent a little
immobile by the bend,
hands in our pockets,
leather handbag
motionless like the low
white clouds over the mountain
at the empty end of the road.

Cold over the Digging Site

Long smooth wooden
backrest
with sleeping tramps
leaning against each other,
level with
well-dressed people
who do not speak
but stare ahead motionless
in the mist,
stare into the cold over the deep
digging site:
loose earth where the men have worked.
Handrails
slanting separating the space,
the grey,
the platform roofs.
Two steps down
you lengthen the underpass,
you cut rectangles out
of white light.

Plucked by the Wind

Plucked by the wind
the bell-tower
suspended seems
in the yellow strange sky
where black wires cross
other tense, remote,
abstract wires.
It sinks with the rest:
with the adorned portal
with the bells...
Or it rises light faraway
plucked by the wind.

A Little More than Mist

A little more than mist,
along outlines of sloping roofs,
rugged like a stain,
all around the square,
like the blocks of flats,
all around
it surrounds the soft pale-greys,
the umbrellas,
people's identical heads.
A little more than mist
the arc of treetops
surrounds the market place.

The Lovers

They threw little liqueur bottles
onto the dark soil of our vegetable garden,
sloping steeply down
to the grey stone roof.
They played, their voices broken
by the sound of water
streaming transparent and silver
from the rusty gutters.
They passed through the smells in the valley:
grey and silver smells
cut by the rain.
They laughed...
I heard them laughing
and I saw the clear, elegant
trajectories of the little empty
transparent bottles.

The Square

Lights out
leaving a pale grey
in the rain,
and black arcades and red roofs
and sharp angles where the cymatia end;
string of modillions marking a clean-cut
perspective of houses,
dullhumans walking
stooping along the diagonals
of the square.

Rust Iron Freshness

The mind's corners are these:
brush on the balustrade,
rust iron freshness
coming from the rubbish,
dusty shutter splinter of wood,
rice from a packet
pecked by sparrows...
A strong scent of water,
a strong sound of rain
I hear,
I do not know what
I do not know how
I smell
a strong sound of rain,
a strong scent of water.
Bull heads
spouting water
where swallows drink.

Dotted with Pebbles

    Far is the land
    of cigarette butts
on the same level
as the book I am holding

    dotted with pebbles
    a halo continuing
    sweeping beyond
my field of vision...

Pale Eyes

Pale eyes
    in suspended beams
staring at men

tender grey skyscrapers
    pale pearls
of faraway air melting
    away.

Crows Black Edges

How they twist
their wooden necks
crows black edges
dangling on swaying
branches

    the table
strewn with objects
spilling the chill
spilling the lights settling
    into space.

Heavy Cart

Heavy cart
on rimmed wheels
iron weighing where
rust-claws crack
the asphalt
     tender rain
crumbling melting
its liquid colour.

It Draws Strength From

It draws strength from
    beyond the frame
the dense ruffled
    leaf-top
    detached from the text
moving apart
with its rhythm
its song.

In the Old Yellow Paint

    Like this but also a shade
where a cone of light opens

    soft rounded flexible
shade bending
    discreetly
in the old yellow paint.

Enamel in Motion

Enamel in motion
on still objects
    peeling off
swelling damp
    for the small
    quiet splashes
of rain.

Story of One

I

    Nesting shadows
    between nose and moustache
and in his beard
    of ice

    he pirouettes madly to smiles
involved thoughts
    behind steel-rimmed glasses
pale sea-green pearls.

II

Holding his face
he deforms it
sinking his thumb
into the big putty
nose
    motionless now
thin moustache
gleaming look
along the sides of his nose
a vacant look
overflowing the
barely perceptible
square
the corners of something.

III

    Stooping whim
    watching the high
    lopsided strolling
    of spiders

thin lips slowly
reciting litanies.

IV

Big odd scorching
sharp-edged sun
orange tiles
lively rectangles skyscrapers
in Fifth Avenue

hanging green rag
and the old man on his
        deathbed
finding a comfortable position
with a small gesture
his shoulders
his chin.

V

Disclose disclose
    disclose yourself
flesh by flesh
    pain for your effort
litter gilt twigs
    framed
glossy
    aged faces
hanging
    in a straight line.

Vertigo on the Ground

I

    Small frenetic
suspended movements
      unresolved gestures

      inside me hanging
      on a nail
      swaying
      fading morning

    careful smooth
morning
    this finite pearl green
    round table.

II

    Annoying fly's
    flight

alone in its crooked
gliding flight

    over a clear reflection
a curious annoying cloud
    moving softly
steeply away.

III

Subtle painful darkness
curling up
    me on the frozen
    step of a door
with its sun handle
touching the nave

    darkness opening on the stained-glass window
in silence in a line
triangles squares circles
between the pews.

IV

     Vertigo on the ground
         drawing hints from the fringes
lopsided backrests
rectangular surfaces

     glances on a level
with bricks
     or along the sides
of my nose to the dry
        edges of the road.

V

They have brought something
that belongs to me
in the light of a drop
that falls

     something I know
I had better
forget the useless effort

home
     once more
home again.

VI

I can go beyond within
match lights with points
    matching lights with points
in the spherical certainty
sweet tiredness,
    fear, eyes
sinking.

Notes

Like Corks Floating Downstream: Balbal is an invented character, similar to the old men in Baudelaire's poems.

Rust Iron Freshness: 'bull heads' are typical fountains in Turin.

Biographical Note

Andrea Bianchi was born in 1960 in Turin (Italy) where he still lives with his wife. He started writing poetry at the age of thirteen, though his creative bent can be traced back to his childhood when he used to invent stories for his friends. His first collection of poems, *La stanza prosegue* (Edizioni del Leone), was published in 1990, followed by *Corvi spigoli neri* (Edizioni del Leone) in 1996, *...sospeso teso / filo di luci...*(Mobydick) in 2002 and *Abracacadarba* (Mobydick) in 2008.

Since 1997 Andrea Bianchi and Silvana Siviero, his Welsh-born wife, have worked as translators. Their series, *Parole dal Galles / Geiriau o Gymru* (Mobydick), created and directed by them, and supported by Wales Literature Exchange, promotes the literatures of Wales. It is unique in Italy and a flagship project for other European countries. They are the founding editors of a unique series of poetry in UK, *Minorities Not Minority: A window on Italian cultures*, forthcoming from Cinnamon Press.

Italian authors who do not speak/write/dream only in Italian but in regional languages such as Sardinian, Friulian etc, reach the world in English thanks to collaboration between Andrea Bianchi, Silvana Siviero and experts from these cultures. They also organise events and festivals to promote the books translated, with special emphasis placed on performance.